W9-CSO-757

The Five Secrets

Dedicated with love, thanks and admiration to Linda, my best friend, teacher and loving partner for almost forty years. Without you, none of this would have ever happened. And for you I am eternally grateful.

Is this what you've been looking for?

You aren't reading this book by accident.

No, you picked it up because you've finally had enough of the old life you've been living. And you're looking for a way that actually works to get "out of your box" and into the new life you're after.

Yes, the one you've been dreaming about for so long!

And you know you've got to do it now because you've realized, for some reason, that you haven't got forever to make this happen.

Maybe the huge changes the world's going through have finally forced you to wake up and realize it's now or never to live your Dream.

Maybe you've had a friend, or someone you know, get sick or die…like that 40-year-old you heard about the other day who dropped dead from a heart attack or the 28-year-old with incurable cancer. Now you know it could happen to you.

Maybe your body's finally had all it can handle and your health's gone bad…and you've got to change the way you've been living so you can, hopefully, get your health back.

Maybe you're tired of spending your life on the road, whispering "Good night, I love you!" to your kids from one hotel room after another, your heart breaking because you *know* they're growing up too fast, *know* you're running out of time, *know* all those birthdays and ball games and special times you're missing will never come again.

Maybe you gave up your life for your job, and now as their way of saying "Thanks!" you've been fired or laid off and you've got to move on, like it or not…and it's harder now because you're older and the competition's tougher.

Maybe you're buried in debt from buying all the stuff that was supposed to make you happy, important and successful, but it's not…and you're ready to give up being an economic slave just to pay the bills for what it takes to keep up with everyone else.

Maybe the life you've been living is simply over, and it's time to move on to something new.

Or maybe, just maybe, you wanna have a little fun before you die and some part of you knows it's now or never.

No, I don't know exactly why you're here, but I do know you're *not* here by accident.

Some part of you knows it's time to get *free*, time to make the changes you've been thinking about making for a long time, time to get the life you *really* want…and it knows you need to do it *now*, while you still can.

That's why you're here.

And the good news is, you *can* do it! You *can* make it happen!

Because the Five Secrets work.

So take a deep breath, relax and let's begin. The answers you've been looking for are here....

Pat Lynch

P.S. Please join me on the web at www.patlynch.com. While you're there, don't forget to register for *Out of the Box*, the free e-mail newsletter designed to help you find more effective ways to release your potential and get the life you've always wanted.

Also by Pat Lynch:

The Five Secrets Companion Journal
A Practical Guide To Getting Free
And Changing Your Life Forever

You Can, Too!
Real Stories By Real People Who Have Gotten
Out Of The Box And Can Show You The Way

The Five Secrets Audio CD
Read by Pat Lynch

The Five Secrets

What You're **NOT** Supposed
To Know Because It Will Set
You Free And Change Your
Life Forever!

Pat Lynch

POTENTIAL PRESS
www.potentialpress.com

Potential Press
1042 Willow Creek Rd., Suite A-101-250
Prescott, Arizona 86301
information@potentialpress.com

The Five Secrets

Copyright © 2003 by Pat Lynch
All rights reserved. No part of this book may be reproduced, used, transmitted,
or stored in any manner or form or by any means whatsoever without the written
permission of the Publisher, except by a reviewer, who may quote brief passages
in a review.

To receive a free weekly e-mail newsletter designed to help you find more
effective ways to release your potential and get the life you want, register directly
at http://www.patlynch.com

Bulk Sales
For information on special discounts for bulk purchases or to learn how your
organization may use this book and include your message in a customized version,
e-mail: information@potentialpress.com

Names, identifying characteristics, facts, and situations have been changed to
protect the privacy of individuals and organizations.

Disclaimer: the purpose of this book is only to offer general information that
helps you in your quest for well-being. In the event you use any of the information
in this book for yourself, which is your constitutional right, the author and the
publisher shall have no liability or responsibility to any person or entity with
respect to any loss or damage caused, or alleged to have been caused, directly or
indirectly, by the information contained in this book.

Library of Congress Control Number: 2003092148

ISBN 0-9728096-7-8

Printed in the United States of America

This book is printed on acid-free paper.

The Five Secrets

Contents

The
Five
Secrets

Secret #1: Wake Up!

It was long past midnight and he sat there, staring out the window, as the screech of the plane's wheels signaled our landing in Los Angeles. "We've got everything that's supposed to make us happy," he said, "but life just sucks! All we ever do anymore is work so we can pay for all the stuff we bought, but we're so far behind now we'll never catch up. My wife and I hardly ever see each other anymore," he whispered softly, tears filling his eyes. "And our kids are bein' raised by daycare…what kinda life is that? I've gotta do something about it," he said, his voice fading into the darkness, "before it's too late…."

"A lie, told often enough, becomes the truth."
V. I. Lenin

Brainwashed

The simple truth is: life can be *so* much better than we've got it! But that's a secret we're not supposed to find out, so that's not the way it turns out for most of us.

Instead of enjoying the life we want, most of us wind up enduring an existence that's barely tolerable.

And we do it…and continue to do it…because most of us have been brainwashed into believing that's the way life is "supposed" to be.

Life, we've been trained to believe, is "supposed" to be hard, "supposed" to be a struggle…and so, of course, that's the way we make it.

Where'd we get such goofy ideas?

Easy: they got pounded into our heads from the moment we were born as the "right way" to live, and we bought them all without question. Born free, we popped into the world clean, like a blank slate.

But we didn't stay that way very long.

Almost immediately the "big people" in our lives and the institutions of whatever culture we were born into began "teaching" us all the "right" beliefs, attitudes, values, fears, and behaviors *(or at least what they believed was "right")*.

And before long we saw the world and everything in it the same way they did. It didn't make any difference whether "their" way was the "best" way or had anything to do with who we were or what we wanted.

It was *their* way and *the* way, and they made sure we bought it.

And so we wound up, as a result, being "boxed" in for the rest of our lives by a bunch of old ways of thinking and being that are now keeping us from getting the "Heaven on Earth" we want – and could easily have – if only we could find the way out.

Locked in the box

But getting out of our "box" and into the life we want is a lot easier said than done because we've been locked in that box most of our life.

You know all those old beliefs, attitudes, values, fears, and behaviors you and I were programmed to believe and live our lives by? The ones that are now keeping us from getting what we want?

Well, grab this: 90% of them were locked into our heads by the time we were 10 years old...and 80% of us never change them.

(Think about that! Most of the people you work with, play with and hang with think pretty much the same way they did when they were 10 years old! Yeah, their bodies are bigger, but their "box," the belief system that controls their life, the one they use to think with and make decisions with, is more often than not that of a 10-year-old child!)

Oh sure, you and I make a few refinements here and there as the years go by and life knocks us around, but the core of who we are and what we believe – our "box" – remains virtually unchanged.

So it's no wonder we make some pretty strange, self-defeating choices...not because we're stupid or thick between the ears, but because our box, our way of seeing the world, stubbornly refuses to change and grow. And because it believes we already know "the truth," it constantly filters all incoming data and screens out *everything* that doesn't fit with what we already believe to be true.

Why should you care?

Because that means you and I are constantly and automatically rejecting most everything that's new or different: if it doesn't fit with what we've been taught to believe is "right" and "true," it never even gets into our heads.

And that creates a major problem for us because the new things we're screening out are the very things we desperately need in order to survive and succeed in today's rapidly changing world.

So we fail, even though we're doing our best, not because we can't win...but because we're trying to use a bunch of tired old options, choices and strategies that aren't working anymore. And, worse, we fail because our box is constantly blinding us to the new and unexpected opportunities that are trying so hard to happen in our lives.

(That's right, the very opportunities you and I have been looking for but can't see...even though they're right there in front of us!)

"Now you listen to me!"

And while that's a huge issue for us because it means our box is destroying our chances for success, it's no problem at all for "them"…for all those often well-intentioned people and institutions who've worked so hard to brainwash us and are still doing their best to keep us locked in our box forever.

Who are they? You know them well, and they usually include our…

- Parents and family members – most of whom rarely miss an opportunity to tell us how the "world isn't safe" and the only way we'll ever survive "out there" is to "play it safe" and live the "same way" they do. *(You know who I'm talking about. No, most of them aren't trying to hurt you…they just want what's best for you and simply can't understand why you'd ever want to live any differently than they do. Their problem is, they've found a way to live that works for them and they've made the mistake of assuming it's also the way that'll work best for you. Unfortunately, they're usually wrong.)*

- Teachers – so many of whom encourage us, on the one hand, to "dream big" and tell us we can "do anything, be anything." And then, on the other, do their best to make us be like everyone else. Think for ourselves? Come up with daring new answers that challenge the status quo? "Don't even think about it!"

- Religious leaders – from every flavor of God who keep telling us how "bad" we are so we'll stay in the box and keep "buying" their particular brand of salvation. *(It's appalling how many of them have turned religion into a "business" and are now "selling" God, the creator of the universe and source of all life and love, as another "product" we can "buy" that'll make our pain go away. Surely God's more important than that!)*
- Employers – who keep telling us we're "empowered" and need to be "loyal" and help the organization succeed. But then, in the next breath, tell us to "shut up, quit thinking and do as you're told" and "if I want your opinion, I'll give it to you!"
- Governments – who work hard to keep us enfeebled with an abundance of absurd rules, regulations, policies, and procedures, most of which are designed to protect the haves from the have-nots and keep things the way they are. *(That's right, most of them believe it's their job to maintain the status quo even though it's obviously killing us.)*
- Media and advertisers – who pay movie stars, super-rich athletes, drugged-out musicians, and some seriously warped people big bucks to push their products and be "role models" for what it takes to be "successful" and live the "good life."

And those are just a *few* of the people who've been standing in line all your life to tell you how you "ought" to be living!

Want to know the real reason most of us never get what we want? The real reason our lives turn into a living hell we endure instead of the Heaven on Earth we could have?

It's because no one told us Secret #1.

No one told us we had to "Wake Up!" and get past the brainwashing and tell ourselves the truth about what was actually happening so we could *really* live and get what we wanted.

So we stayed asleep and bought all the nonsense "they" told us. And we're still buying it because they're still brainwashing us, still pumping those same life-limiting messages into our heads every day of our lives.

But most of us would rather live with all those illusions and lies than wake up and tell ourselves the truth about what's really going on…and change.

"Do not wake me up!"

So we choose, whether we realize it or not, to stay asleep in our same little box and keep things the way they are.

Makes no difference we're dying here or that life sucks or we're miserable: most of us stubbornly cling to the same old thinking that's ruining our days and blowing our chances for a life worth living. And we keep trying to make it all okay by telling everyone who'll listen the same stupid lie "they" told us, the same one that's *still* screwing up our life:

> *"This is just the way things are and how
> they're going to be, and there's nothing we
> can do about it."*

But as much as we'd like to believe that self-defeating nonsense is true, the good news is…*we are completely wrong!*

Because the truth is, we have all the power we need to make our life be any way we'd like it. All we've got to do is dump most of the old thinking that got brainwashed into our head and now has us locked up tight in that little box we call "our life."

(About now, if you're normal, your box is probably screaming, "That's wrong! That's not the way life works at all! I know what's right and this guy's full of it…put this book down right now and stick with me! I'll tell you what's best for you!" But, of course, if that's true, why

isn't your life already working better than it is? Why are you reading this book right now? I know this is probably hard to hear, but your box is wrong. No, your life doesn't have to be the way it is. And yes, you can get out of your box and get what you want. The only real question is: will you wake up and do it?)

Dumbing down, drifting and dozing

So here we are…

Bright, talented, with more potential than we'll ever use and more opportunities than we know what to do with…

And we're stuck.

Because we got brainwashed and wound up believing a bunch of myths, illusions and outright lies that now have us locked into a tiny life that's slowly killing us.

And while it's hard to believe any of us are gullible enough to fall for all of that, the truth is we *all* buy it…and we *keep* buying it!

Because the brainwashing by the culture never ends.

Day after day we swim in the same old never-ending river of illusions, stupidities, nonsense, and lies that flow, nonstop, from our friends, the media, experts, bosses, churches, teachers, and people we trust.

And day-by-day we slowly, but surely, become just like them…just like all those people who feed us all that garbage…while the Great Self inside us, the person we *really* are, screams for us to learn Secret #1 and "Wake up!" before it's too late.

"You're more than you think you are!" it practically screams. "You can *do* more, *be* more, *have* more! You *can* make your Dream come true! It's all there, waiting for you, if you'll just wake up and get out of your box!"

But the roar of the river of illusions is usually too loud...and we're usually too close to it to hear...and we'd rather not know anyway because we've been trained from birth to forget how special we are.

So we drift off down the same old river, believing the same old stupid lie:

> *"This is all there is...you're nothing spe-*
> *cial...give up your crazy Dream...be like*
> *everyone else...then we'll love you."*

And so, of course, that's exactly what most of us do.

Choosing *(yes, choosing)* to stay asleep, we give up, dumb down and begin playing the same old "buy as much as you can" game everyone else is playing. And, like them, wind up buried under a staggering pile of bills and life-limiting obligations, selling our soul for more of what usually doesn't matter, doing more of what we hate so we can make enough money, and spending our days and nights trying to find ways to make the pain and emptiness go away...

...because the Great Self inside us, who we really are, *knows* it doesn't have to be this way! *Knows* there's more! *Knows* life's a lot better on the outside of this little jail of a box we've allowed ourselves to be trapped in!

And it wants out now!

(But that's not something most of us are willing to do until we hurt so badly we've got to. What about you? How much more are you going to have to hurt before you'll finally let yourself wake up and get out of your old box and get the life you really want? It's funny...the pain we keep trying to avoid becomes our best friend because it's the only force strong enough to make us wake up, take charge of our lives and do what we need to do to get what we want. Who'd a thought?)

And the fish asked, "What water?"

But most of us don't even know we're living in a box.

We haven't got a clue that every facet of our existence is being controlled by an old belief system that we don't even know exists!

Talk with most of us, and it's like swimming under water and gliding up next to a talking fish *(you'll have to use a little imagination here)* and asking the fish, "What's it like to live in the water?"

"Water?" the fish replies, "*What* water?" Because it doesn't know "water" exists, or that "water" is controlling its life.

And you, of course, are shocked!

"*This* water!" you gurgle, bubbles streaming from your mouth. "Can't you see it? It's right here in front of your gills!" But the fish, rather than seeing what's so obvious to you, looks at you like you're crazy and swims off, convinced it's had a close encounter with a creature who's obviously half a flipper off.

Because it can't see the water!

Makes no difference that water controls its life and everything it does and all it becomes; the water itself is invisible because it's *everywhere*. The fish doesn't even know it's there!

Same thing happens with us and our box.

Sure, it controls every part of our life.

But ask most of us about "our box" and you get the same blank stare you got from the fish who wondered what in the name of Neptune you were talking about.

"Box?" we ask, "*what* box?"

Because we can't see it...since it's everywhere... which makes it as invisible to us as the water is to the fish.

And even though our "box" determines and limits *what* we do and *how* we do it and *when* and *why* we do it and *who* we become and what's "normal," it continues on, unquestioned, and causes all kinds of things to happen or not happen, much of which makes us miserable...because we don't know it's there.

Don't know *that's* what's been screwing up our life.

Don't know *that's* why we hurt so bad.

And don't know *that's* why nothing will ever change for us, despite our hard work and good intentions, until we finally learn Secret #1 and wake up and set ourselves free.

Going nowhere fast!

But getting out of the box we've been living in is hard because our culture and most everyone in it are doing their best to keep us *in* the box, "playing the game."

Why?

Well, to begin with, you and I are easier to control if we're locked into playing the same old "Pay, Play and Obey" game as everyone else. If the folks in charge can keep us doing that, they're guaranteed a steady supply of lifelong wage slaves.

(You know, "nice little people" who show up and do as they're told and put in their time and get a check every couple of weeks and take a short vacation once a year. That's who we've been brainwashed into believing we're "supposed" to be! Get free, do your own thing, run your own life, get a job you love that works for you? Get real! You're supposed to be like everyone else and struggle to make ends meet. Getting out of your box and actually living is NOT part of their plan!)

The other reason the folks running the game want to keep us playing is because that guarantees them a huge and easily manipulated market of consumers for all the stuff they're selling that's making them wealthy.

You know, pills and potions and cars and clothes and $3-a-cup coffee and all the other stuff we keep buying to dull the pain that comes from being locked up tight in a life that all-too-often simply sucks.

("You say your life's not working? No problem! Buy a new SUV or a cruise or a tummy tuck or a new house or get on Prozac or Viagra...that'll make you happy!" And that works for a while, but before long most of us are back out there looking for "what's next" because what we've bought just "isn't doing it" for us anymore. Pavlov would laugh at how well we've been brainwashed to "buy stuff" so we'll be happy.)

But these are things most of us playing the game don't really want to know or admit, so we wind up staying locked in our same old box forever.

And all we see and hear, as the culture relentlessly pounds its same old beliefs into our heads, is one message after another trying to keep us playing the same old Pay, Play and Obey Game:

- **Pay** – be like everyone else and buy all the stuff you can, regardless of whether you need it, want it or can afford it, because "the more you have, the happier you'll be!" *(And you've got to hand it to them: they even say all that self-serving nonsense with a straight face, like they actually believe it!)*

- **Play** – and when life gets tough because you're doing all the stuff "they" told you to do but it's only making things worse, well, keep doing it anyway! Get out of your box? Make different choices? Live differently? Follow your Dream? Nahhh! The folks running the game don't want you doing that because it'll cut into their profits. "Be more hopeful!" they tell us. "It'll all work out." *(Yeah, right, for them.)*

- **Obey** – finally, we're all supposed to keep being "good little boys and girls" who "do as we're told" by all those self-serving authorities in our lives who keep trying to control us "for our own good." Come into our own power and take charge of our lives and do what we know is best? That'll never happen if they have their way because they've deluded themselves into thinking they know what's best for us. *(And they will, I promise you, do whatever it takes to gag the Great Self inside you so you'll keep following their same old stupid rules and stay locked in your box forever.)*

"Just be like everyone else!"

Yet as self-defeating as the Pay, Play and Obey Game is, they're still able to get most of us to buy in and go along with it because they use the people we care about most to keep selling it to us.

(You know, family, friends, people we trust, believe in, follow....)

"We're only telling you these things because we care about you," these people whisper in our ear. "We just want what's best for you! Come on, relax, lighten up, be like everybody else."

"Be a good little girl/boy who goes along and gets along and doesn't make waves. Be polite and politically correct and do all the *right* things you're *supposed* to do...oh, you're so good when you're like that! See, isn't life better this way? Now listen, don't you ever have those crazy thoughts again and you'll be happy!"

(Ugh! It's enough to make your skin crawl!)

So, of course, that's exactly what most of us do.

And before we know it, we've become "just like everybody else" and we're doing "what everybody else does"...

...as we treadmill our way through a pill-popping life, stuffing ourselves with everything we can find that promises to make the pain inside us go away and the voice inside us shut up...the voice of our Great Self that keeps screaming:

"For God's sake, wake up! This isn't you! You're not just another one of the walking dead! You're special! There's more – wake up!"

(Take a minute right now and ask yourself: who in your life has been telling you to "be like everyone else" and trying to keep you in your box? Who's been trying to get you out? Which of them have you been listening to and why? Where will you wind up if you don't choose to get out now?)

Sex, drugs and rock & roll

But the voice of our Great Self becomes weaker the faster we run and the more we work and drink and drug and eat and shop and have sex and travel and bungee jump...*whatever it takes* to smother the voice of our Great Self, to shut it up so we don't have to listen to it anymore.

And finally the day comes when we realize it's happened...we're doing so much and moving so fast we can hardly hear the voice...

...because our locked-on-fast-forward life has now spun out of control and we've become like everyone else...

...swamped with nonstop e-mails, phone calls, voice mails, faxes, insane schedules, absurd deadlines, obsessed people, and endless meetings, our chain constantly being jerked 24 hours a day, 7 days a week by someone, somewhere, the stress not-so-quietly killing us...

...as we incessantly chase money and power and things and discover – usually too late – that we've blown off our health, the people who love us and most everything else that really matters.

And still, in the midst of it all, our Great Self struggles to wake us up...until, finally, it gives up and goes off to sleep as the relentless hammering of the media nails our box shut thousands of times a day with commercial messages from the Culture telling us to keep Paying, Playing and Obeying.

And so, of course, most of us do...and wind up locked in our box till we die.

"Stuff" happens!

Unless something big happens!

Like…we get fired or laid off or one of our kids gets hurt badly. A wreck on the freeway slams us into a guardrail and slaps us into a body cast. Our marriage tanks, one of our partners embezzles all the money, the economy craps out, or maybe we have a heart attack one nice afternoon on our way back from lunch.

You know, something big and ugly and terrible and massively painful…because that's the kind of heavy-duty pain it usually takes to break the grip of our old belief system and kick us out of our box.

And *that's* when the pain we've tried so hard to run away from becomes our best friend as it reaches for us through the wreckage of our whacked-out life and tells us, quietly, in a voice that will no longer be denied:

> *"No more! It's time now to wake up! Time*
> *to remember who you really are! Time to*
> *let your Great Self out of this damnable*
> *box and get on with doing your Dream!"*

And so we agree…not because we want to, but because we know, in that part of us where the lies stop and the truth lives, that there's no other way out.

No other way to make our terrible pain go away.

The Awakening

So we begin.

And it's hard ripping off the old blinders we've worn for so long, hard to wake up and see, often for the first time, who we are and what's really happening to us.

Hard to tell ourselves the truth we've always known but never wanted to admit. Because we knew if we let ourselves know…that would change everything.

"Who am I?" we wonder as we question everything we've been told and believed, from the most sacred to the most profane.

"Is this *it*? Is this *all* there is? What's *my* life all about? What's true for *me*? What do *I* want and how do I get it? Why'd I put up with all that crap for so long and not do anything about it?"

No longer willing to blindly accept the teachings, rants and preachings of our families, churches, bosses, governments, institutions, companies, experts, consultants, talking heads and gurus, we begin searching for what's true for *us*.

And that truly ticks off the folks in charge…who only get to keep their money, power and prestige if they can keep us asleep, Paying, Playing and Obeying.

What do they say when we begin to wake up and think for ourselves?

"You've changed! I just don't know who you are anymore!" *(Like that's a bad thing?)*

"Have you lost your mind?" they scream, followed quickly by "You are so –" *(check all that apply)* "– stupid, lazy, idiotic, and such a loser, screw-up, slacker, goofball, bum, dork, heretic, or *(fill in your favorite)*."

"You're so selfish!" By now their arms are usually flailing, eyes bulging, voice cracking as they break into a rant: "All you care about's yourself! Just who do you think you are? What would happen if everybody lived like that!" *(If you're up for a little fun, smile and answer, "They'd all be happy!" and watch 'em freak.)*

"You're going to –" *(check all that apply)* "– die, go broke, lose everything, get sick, go to hell, burn your bridges, screw up your credit, lose your job, go to jail, get blackballed, be all alone, lose your mind, make me cry!"

Whatever it takes to make you stop changing!

Because if they can't stop you, the game will be over for them as far as you're concerned. You'll be free!

And they won't have any more power left over you or what you do because you'll be awake…and on your way out of the box…knowing, finally, the truth: there *is* a Good Life and you've got whatever it takes to make it happen!

What's stopping you?

So what, exactly, does this box that's holding you back look like?

What old beliefs, attitudes, values, fears, and behaviors make up its walls and keep you from getting exactly what you want?

The easiest way to find out is by going through the following list of the most common ones, checking off all those that describe you and adding those that are uniquely yours.

(I know we're starting to get personal here, but I hope you won't let that stop you. We're all – yes, all – boxed-in by walls of one kind or another, and the easiest way to break through them is to know what they are. So just tell yourself the truth and remember: this information's private and not meant to be shared with anyone.)

Usual beliefs, attitudes, values, fears, and behaviors that keep us boxed in:
(Check all that apply)

❏ "I'm a victim of forces beyond my control"
❏ "I'm not (good, smart, strong, etc.) enough"
❏ Focus on the urgent vs. the important
❏ Think others know best, will take care of me
❏ Play it safe, don't risk; hate making mistakes
❏ Don't like change; keep doing what's worked
❏ Keep my mouth shut; maintain a low profile
❏ Wait to act until I'm told what to do
❏ Let others control me
❏ Feel overly responsible for others
❏ Am rigid, predictable and consistent
❏ Focused on making a living vs. making a life
❏ Emotionally flat, little energy, monotone
❏ Don't see trends, changes, the big picture
❏ Feel bound by others' rules and expectations
❏ Controlled by my past, by history, tradition
❏ Unsure of myself and my abilities
❏ Focus on what can go wrong; worry a lot
❏ Fear failing, succeeding, the future, being ridiculed, rejected, hurt, etc.
❏ Won't fully commit; always hold back a little
❏ Driven to look good; need others' approval
❏ Complain and whine a lot
❏ Afraid I'll lose control, screw up, look bad, lose my job, power, prestige, friends, etc.
❏ Other? _____
❏ Other? _____

Now describe your box in 50 words or less, and be sure to include the dominant beliefs, values, attitudes, fears, and behaviors that are keeping you from getting what you want. *(I know this is hard...make it easy on yourself by just telling it like it is and remembering you're the only one who'll ever see it.)*

_____

_____

_____

_____

_____

_____

_____

_____

What are the two strongest fears (walls) holding you back? What are you going to do about them? When? Why?

_____

_____

_____

_____

_____

_____

_____

_____

Secret #2: Remember Who You Really Are

*"Think you're pretty hot stuff, don't ya," the
angry old man growled at the little boy. "Well,
I'll tell you who you are. You're nothin' special,
that's who, and don't you ever forget it!"*
And he never did.

Getting out of your box and living the life you've always wanted depends on how you choose *(yes, choose)* to answer one simple question:

Who do you think you are?

Ask most of us that question and you get pretty much the same answer.

"Me?" we gasp, trying to find a way to disappear into the floor. "I'm not much, nobody special."

Pressed for more of an answer than that, most of us finally tell it the way we've been taught to see it: "Really, there's nothing special about me...I'm pretty much like everybody else," we practically whisper, shaking our head left and right, hoping they'll shut up and quit asking.

And the tragedy is most of us actually believe all that garbage about ourselves! *(Yes, even people who act cool and try hard to convince us they've got it all together!)*

Why *do* we think so little of ourselves? Why do we work so hard to be *less* than we are? Why have we forgotten how good we are? And why do we refuse to stand apart from the crowd, let our power out and create what we *really* want from life?

The reason, as you've probably guessed by now, boils down to the simple fact that most of us have been brainwashed from birth into believing the huge and terrible lie that we're just "not much."

Believe in ourselves and our potential? Admit to our own greatness? Dare to stand apart from the herd and be who we really are and go for our Dreams?

Not going to happen for most of us.

No, not because we can't do it…but because we *won't* do it.

Why? Because we've been trained all our lives to play a game called "Conform!" How? By being like everyone else, fitting in, following the rules, playing it safe, doing as we're told, taking very few risks, refusing to think for ourselves, keeping a low profile, and doing whatever it takes to look good and be liked, loved, accepted, and appreciated by others.

That's the game we're supposed to play because that's the game "everybody else" is playing, and our brainwashing is clear: we need to "conform" because we're "not much," and we need the group because there's no way we can make it on our own.

Put simply, fitting in and being liked by everyone else is a lot more important than being ourselves and living the Dream we're here to do.

That's the lie the "big people" told us as we were growing up, and it's the same lie they're still telling us today.

No wonder most of us have forgotten how good we are and settled for an existence that's so much less than the life we could have and, quite frankly, deserve.

But that's a life you'll never get to have until you learn Secret #2 and remember, finally, who you really are and accept the fact that you are...*exceptional!*

(I know it's probably hard to hear that, but you're going to have to face reality sometime and it might as well be now. Trust me, if you keep arguing for being less than you are, you're going to get to keep the life you've already got. If that's not what you've got in mind, then this is the perfect time to begin accepting your own greatness and living your life accordingly.)

That's right – the truth you were never supposed to discover is that you're smarter than you think, more resourceful than you realize, have more power, control and potential than you imagine, and can accomplish far more than you ever thought possible.

That's who you really are...everything else you've been told is a lie!

The other truth you've got to accept is the fact that you're here to do the Dream that keeps playing in your head *(yes, that one you keep thinking about)*, and you've got – or can get – literally everything you need to make it actually happen.

All you've got to do is wake up, remember how good you are, decide what you want, commit, and then do it!

(Yes, it's that simple!)

Play "The Game"...or else!

But that's not what the "big people" told most of us while we were growing up.

Why? Because they'd been brainwashed, too. Trained by *their* parents, teachers, preachers, and friends to believe *they* were less than they were and locked-up tight in the same old Pay, Play and Obey box with everyone else.

So they, of course, did what they'd been taught was "right" and brainwashed us into the same old life-limiting belief system they were stuck in, honestly believing they had an *obligation* and *responsibility* to make certain we "believed the truth" and "lived our lives the right way."

Did they do it because they cared about us and thought that was what was best for us?

Usually.

But they also did it because they wanted to make sure you and I kept playing the game...that we didn't quit and go off and do our own thing and follow our Dreams and screw *their* life up. Because that's what happens when we refuse to go along and fit in and be like everyone else...and that's why all the folks playing the game work so hard to make sure you keep on playing.

As for you being your "unique self" and following "your Dream" and making "your life worth living" by "doing your own thing"?

Forgetaboutit!

Your job is to conform…to follow *their* rules…meet *their* expectations…play *their* game…and forget *your* "childish" Dreams.

(And we, unfortunately, make the same demands of most of the people in our lives who are trying to get out of their box and get a life worth living. How thrilled are you, for example, when your daycare provider wants to quit and do "her Dream"? Or when your husband, wife, kids, parents, or friends decide to quit doing the things you've counted on them for and make a change? Right…forgetaboutit!)

What really matters to most people is that you and I keep doing what we've always done so *their* life keeps working.

Don't forget that.

And realize that when you try and change the game that's been working for them, try and break out of the same old box they're locked into, you're going to get threats, fights, name calling, guilt, screaming, even the silent treatment…whatever it takes to keep you playing the game so *they* won't have to change.

"You don't love me anymore!" they'll wail, or "I won't love you anymore!" or "I can't believe you're doing this to me after all I've done for you!" or "I just want what's best for you!"

You're going to hear all that and more until *(they hope)* you finally give up and agree to keep playing the same old stupid game that's slowly killing you…

…as you trudge through one miserable day after another, mumbling, "It's not so bad. I can put up with it."

And nothing's going to change until you wake up and remember who you *really* are, stand up for yourself and your Dream, and tell the people who've been running your life for way too long:

"It's over! No more! I quit!"

Until you do, you'll stay part of the herd and spend your days running scared, sucking up and humoring and tolerating the "powers that be"...

> ...as you do your best to stay out of harm's way and not tick anyone off...

> ...and work hard to make the folks in charge richer...

> ...while you follow the rules *they made up*...

> ...to keep you playing the game that's working for *them!*

Enough!

But it doesn't have to be that way…if you're willing to quit playing their games and buying their lies that you're less than you are. And accept, finally, the simple truth of Secret #2 that you were never supposed to find out because it'd set you free forever: you *are* exceptional!

Yes, you *are* better than you think you are.

Yes, you have more power and control than you realize.

Yes, you can do, be and have more than you ever thought possible. That's just what's true.

And you can have whatever you want if you're willing to accept your own greatness and take charge of your own life and make it happen.

(I know, I said the "g" word again – greatness. Don't get turned off…that's just what's so, and you've got to accept that about yourself or you're doomed to stay locked in your box forever. Listen, God doesn't make junk! You're NOT some sniveling little nothing! You are special, whether you want to believe it or not, and you've got more potential than you'll ever use. It's all right there inside you, just waiting for you to wake up, take back your power and run your own life. Which, as you've probably guessed by now, is the only way you'll ever get what you want. The next time you get discouraged, feel unsure of yourself, get lost or confused, re-read Secret #2 and remember the truth of who you really are and get back on track.)

So what's great about you?

That's right, *you*...what's *your* greatness? What's *special* about you?

No, you don't have to be famous or lead the country or cure cancer or free mankind.

The greatness I'm talking about comes from being the Great Self that God created *you* to be, whoever that is, and giving your unique gifts to the world, whatever they are. So drop your modesty for a few minutes, grab a pen and tell yourself the truth about who you really are *(yes, you do know...you may not want to admit it, but you do know).*

This is what's special about me:

_____

_____

_____

_____

_____

_____

_____

_____

_____

_____

_____

_____

Secret #3: Take Control!

"If you were an animal," they asked a bunch of kids and adults, "would you rather live in the wild where it's dangerous and you had to find your own food and water, or would you rather live in the zoo, behind a fence, where they'd take good care of you and give you food and water every day and people would come and stare at you?" The kids chose to live in the wild, but most of the adults chose to live in the zoo and came up with a hundred "good reasons" why they had "no other choice."

Let me out of here!

But "taking control" feels so strange, so weird, so abnormal!

("What do you mean 'take control,'" your box may well be saying right now. "I am in control of my life!" But if that was true, I doubt you'd be here reading this.)

I mean, think about it: you and I have been brainwashed all our lives into believing that someone else has our answers, that someone else has to give us their permission, that someone else knows what's best for us and all we've got to do is do it and quit asking why.

Now we're supposed to learn Secret #3 and quit asking for their approval and give ourselves permission to do whatever we think is best?

Bizarre!

And because that feels so strange, so uncomfortable, so wrong, most of us choose *not* to do it.

Repeat, we *choose* not to do it.

Not because we can't, but because we won't.

"What would *they* think?" most of us ask ourselves, panic filling our brain as we half-scream, "I can't do that!"

So rather than take control and run our own life, most of us choose to give up.

To settle.

To take the path of least resistance and give up our Dream and being true to ourself.

And choose, instead, to be just like everyone else.

To stay with the same old brainwashing and spend the rest of our days believing the same old fantasy that "someone else" knows what's best for us, and "they'll" take good care of us.

The YoYo Revolution

But that old strategy of expecting someone else to take care of us and make our Dreams come true simply doesn't work anymore in the real world.

Hard work, self-sacrifice, loyalty, putting yourself last, giving your power away to others and expecting them to do what's best for you will get you squat in today's world.

(Actually, less than squat because it'll make sure you stay an economic slave!)

The only rule that works anymore? *YoYo!* Which stands for: "You're On Your Own!"

Want a better job? Promotion? Your own business? New car? House? More money? Better credit? Relationships that actually work? A life that's closer to God?

Great...use the power in Secret #3 and take control and make it happen...because it's all up to you!

(Sorry, I didn't make up the rules...that's just the way things work now.)

You – *yes, you!* – are now a free agent, whether you want to be or not, and your job is to take total responsibility for making your own life work. *(Yes, all of it!)*

And that includes selling your services to whoever will give you the most of what you want for them and then moving on when things no longer work for *you.*

(The key word here is "you." Let go and move on when things no longer work for "you." No, that doesn't always mean you're being selfish or a quitter...there's just a time when things are over and it's self-destructive to keep holding on. And you know, instinctively, when that time has come, so trust yourself.)

That's the new reality.

But that way of thinking and acting is often too hard for most of us to actually *do.* So rather than take charge and change our life and get what we want, most of us choose to keep believing our illusions and fantasies and the happy little lies we tell ourselves, and we hope life will get better...

...which seldom happens...

...unless we're lucky and something big comes along and smacks us hard enough to make us wake up and realize the Secret: no one's coming to save us and nothing's going to change until we take control of our life and make our own Dream happen.

"If it's to be...."

That's when most of us finally gather up our courage and make the radically different choice that changes our life forever.

Refusing to spend the rest of our days whining *("Oh God, why did this have to happen to me?" is the all-time favorite)*, we choose, instead, to take back our power – the power that's been there all along – and use it to run our own lives.

How?

By choosing to live, from this moment on, by eight simple little words:

"If it's to be, it's up to me!"

No more whining, moaning, groaning, bellyaching, or bitching.

No more excuses or complaining or pretending that we're the "poor, helpless victim" whose fate is somehow controlled by "circumstances beyond our control" or "the powers that be" or our parents or whoever or whatever else we've been blaming for not getting what we want.

From now on, we're taking total personal responsibility for doing whatever we've got to do to make our own Dream happen...because we've finally got it: Prince Charming's not coming and neither is Superman, the Tooth Fairy, Spiderman, or Santa Claus.

From now on, we've got to be our own superhero and save ourselves by doing whatever it takes.

Now the only real question is: are you willing to do that?

(Nothing in this book is more important than making this one simple choice, because your entire future and all your Dreams depend on whether or not you decide to take control of your own life and run it for yourself. If you choose to do that, mean it and live accordingly, you WILL get what you want. If you don't, you'll get to listen to yourself whine for the rest of your life. Not a pretty sound.)

The Turning Point

So now you've got a decision to make: how do you choose to spend the rest of your life? And you've got two choices *(yes, just two)*.

Choice #1: You can choose to spend it being the Master of your own destiny.

If you make that choice, you're saying you're tired of not getting what you want and you're through taking and making excuses. You're also through putting up with people who spend their lives whining and complaining…including yourself. And you're no longer willing to become involved in other people's silly little games, soap operas, dramas, pettiness, and pretense.

Beginning immediately, you will quit arguing for your limitations and waiting for the "right circumstances" to show up. If they're not there when you need them, you'll create them.

Make this choice and you're saying you're finally willing to believe in yourself and your Dream, accept your power and let yourself have what you've always wanted.

And you refuse – *refuse!* – to ever give up until you get it!

(You have to be wondering about now if there could possibly be another choice. Unfortunately, the answer is yes.)

Choice #2: You can choose to spend your life pretending to be the poor, helpless victim.

And while you'd think nobody in their right mind would choose anything that hurts that bad or works that poorly, you'd be wrong…because the "victim" choice is the one most of us make and remake every day of our lives.

Why?

Because *(you guessed it)* we've been brainwashed all our lives to believe and act like we're the "powerless victim" of forces beyond our control.

And if you're not sure that's true, just take a look at all the people you know and ask yourself: how many of them are honestly running their own life? You know, calling their own shots, living life on *their* terms, making their own Dreams come true?

How many of them are truly in control of their own destiny?

Got it?

Good. Now ask yourself how many of the people you know spend their days enduring life, doing a job they hate, complaining nonstop about their personal soap opera, and whining about "who's" doing "what" to them.

I know it's not much fun to admit...but most of us are stuck in the "victim" box and spend our days rationalizing it as "the only thing I can do" and "the way it has to be." And we honestly believe that silliness is true!

So rather than let ourselves become *too* happy and successful, we choose to curl up in the fetal position in our "safe" little box and "make the best" of rotten situations we should have changed a long time ago.

We run scared and play it safe so we don't get hurt and spend our days trying to find ways to make the pain go away.

And we tell everyone who'll listen how we "just can't understand" why our life's not working!

(It'd almost be funny if it weren't so sad...so many bright people with so much going for them arguing so desperately to keep their old brainwashing and be less than they are. But it doesn't have to be that way.)

Do you want out?

So now you need to decide: will you be the Master or the victim?

Will you be happy, satisfied and successful? Or would you rather spend the rest of your life waiting in vain for someone to come along and save you?

It's your choice...choose now, once and forever:

❑   I'm the Master of my own destiny and I'll run my own life, thank you!

❑   I'm the poor, helpless victim of circumstances beyond my control and that will never change. I give up.

Secret #4: Follow Your Dream

"Tell me: what are you 'supposed' to do with your life? What path are you 'supposed' to follow? Is that your Dream or does it really belong to someone else?"

It's time!

If you're still here *(and I hope you are!)*, I'm guessing you've chosen to be the Master of your own destiny and live life on *your* terms.

And that means learning Secret #4 and committing, once and for all, to doing *your* Dream.

That's right, *your* Dream…the one you've been thinking about for sooooo long…the one that keeps playing in your head…the one that never goes away.

And it could be anything…

…traveling around the world, starting your own business, spending more time with the people you love, getting the job you've always wanted, moving to a small town and slowing down, becoming an artist, moving to the city and making it big, going back to school, becoming a rock star, staying home with your kids, getting out of debt, having enough money to do the things you've always wanted, growing closer to God.

Doesn't make any difference what it is: all that matters is that it's *your* Dream and it's meant to come true *(which is why you have it)*. And it's now time to make it real by taking the next step and deciding your old life's finally over and you *will* create the new one you're after…whatever it takes.

(That's right… "whatever it takes"…because that's the only way your Dream's ever going to happen. And just so we're clear here, I'm not talking about doing anything illegal or immoral or equally stupid. I'm simply saying you've got to be totally committed to your Dream or it's not going to happen, and you're going to have to get real and be willing to make some changes.)

Which means giving up wishing and hoping and conning yourself with illusions of winning the Powerball or receiving a big, juicy inheritance or believing your boss will finally recognize your worth or expecting someone else to take care of you.

Ain't gonna happen!

I don't care how badly you want it to or how many magic charms you carry or potions you drink or what you smoke or how many hours you spend on your knees praying…in the real world, you're going to have to save yourself from a dead-end life.

And that means you've got to give up being patient and quit waiting for the right circumstances to show up or the right people, economy, horoscope, partner, or anything else to wander into your life.

None of that's guaranteed to come along and save you!

The only thing you can count on is deciding and committing that whatever it means and whatever it takes, you hereby give up your old life and take total and complete responsibility for creating the new one you want.

No more excuses, no giving it your "best shot," no "trying," whining, wimping out, waiting, or giving up. You now commit, completely, that you'll either succeed ...or fail miserably and look like an idiot.

(I know that sounds harsh, but that's what works: you refuse to give yourself a way out! You set it up so it's all or nothing, sink or swim, win or lose. And if you think I'm being overly dramatic here, trust me: there will come a time in your life-change process when you will give up unless you're totally committed and unless you've set it up, ahead of time, so you can't escape without making your life completely miserable and looking like a schmuck and a complete loser.)

Then you'll make your Dream happen!

Because you'll have no other choice.

So the answer is being "totally committed" and willing to "do whatever it takes" to make "it" happen.

What does that mean, exactly?

It means you may have to give up being poor and let yourself get rich.

(Don't laugh! Most people won't let themselves get that far out of their box. "Living little" is what their life's always been about, whether they know it or not, and they'll fight you to the death to keep things the way they are...even though they whine about it all the time.)

You may have to quit your job. Move. Get married, divorced or bring an old relationship back to life *(yes, maybe even that one)*. You'll probably have to get organized and work hard, consistently...or, strangely, you may have to step back, quit pushing the river, get out of your own way, and "let go and let God."

(Because it's usually "us" who keeps stopping "us" from getting what we want, no one else.)

You may have to start saving money or quit being so cheap. Give up being right or start trusting your own knowing. Say "No!" to things you don't want to do or start saying "Yes!" Begin opening yourself up or become more private. Get out of debt or borrow more money and use it to create the new life you're after.

You may even *(brace yourself)* have to give up feeling unfulfilled and actually let yourself be happy!

(What a concept!)

I don't know what it'll take for you, but I do know this: you'll be forced, as you go through this process, to get out of your box, out of your comfort zone...because that's where your Dream's at and that's where you're going to have to go to get it.

Which means you've got to decide whether or not you're willing to do "whatever it takes!" to get out of your box and make it happen.

And just as no one else can make that choice for you, no one else can do the work for you, either.

It'll have to be *you* who stands up for your life, tells the world how it's going to be for you from now on, takes the heat, and wins whatever prize you choose. And you'll have to do most of it by yourself because almost no one will stand in line to cheer you on.

Precious few, including your family and best friends, will actively support you in getting out of the same old box they're stuck in and have no intention of leaving.

So if you want a life that's pure magic, one you can't wait to wakeup to and live every day of your life, you're going to have to be the one who makes it happen. And you need to decide whether you're *that* committed to making this Dream of yours happen…by making another choice that will also change your life forever.

Your options?

Choice #1: You commit to doing *whatever it takes* to get your Dream. No more "thinking about it" or wasting time. No more pretzeling yourself into that tiny little box that's not-so-slowly killing you. You're committed to getting out and getting out now!

Choice #2: Nahhh! You'd rather be like everybody else, keep things like they are and spend the rest of your days trying to find ways to make the pain go away while you think about what "could have been" if only you'd had a little more courage and belief in yourself.

Choose now, once and forever:

❑ I commit to doing whatever it takes
    to get my Dream.
❑ Forgetaboutit!

Name it and claim it

So tell me, assuming you've chosen to do "whatever it takes" *(you've come this far...I can't even imagine you'd quit on yourself now)*: how does it feel to have decided, once and for all, that you *are* going to jump out of your box and do whatever it takes to get the life you want?

If you're like most of us who've done it, the answer could easily be "scared to death!" Because most everyone who's ever made that choice has made it the same way: teeth clinched, back against the wall and often with more than a little diarrhea.

I wish it didn't work like that, but it usually does.

The good news is, you'll get over it and things will be fine...as long as you keep moving! Acting! Doing things to make your future happen!

Sit on your butt, hang out, hope things will improve, wish for more, spend your time telling your friends about all the grand things you're going to do, or waste your time expecting miracles to happen without much effort on your part...and you'll fail. *(The old saying is right: "God helps those who help themselves.")*

Because talk counts for nothing in making your new life happen.

Nada, zip, zero.

Action is all that matters! Lots of it. Day in, day out, whether you feel like doing it or not. And the first "action" you need to take is to get crystal clear and very specific about what your Dream actually is and what you want your life to look like.

Repeat: *your* Dream and *your* life!

"It's you, baby, and no one else!"

Because I don't care what your father wants of you or what your mother, brother, sister, aunts, uncles, grandparents, teachers, preacher, friends, or anyone else wants or thinks you "ought" to do, be or have.

None of that matters in the least!

(You need to re-read that sentence at least three times, because what condemns most of us to a life that seriously sucks is trying to live a life that belongs to someone else. Which is what happens when we do what "they" think we ought to do instead of what WE want to do. Most of us make that mistake and then "just can't understand" why our life's not working!)

All I care about – and all you've got to care about – is what *you* want for you.

Because you're not them and they're not you.

You're unique, and your job in this life is to be yourself, regardless of who that is. You are *not* here to try and become a clone of someone else.

And if you think I'm being awfully dogmatic about all this, you're right…I am. Because I know the only way you're ever going to be happy and fulfilled and successful, regardless of how you define it, is to be yourself, whatever it costs.

(Some part of you has to be going ballistic right now because this has to fly in the face of everything you've ever been told is true, right and holy. Hang in, stay open and remember: every great truth was once a great heresy that people refused to believe. They even killed each other, for example, to keep their old beliefs that the sun revolved around the earth and the earth was flat! Both of which, incidentally, aren't nearly as absurd as you trying to live your life according to someone else's idea of "what's right.")

So that means finding *your* Dream, *your* passion, *your* cause, what turns *you* on.

It means discovering what you're already naturally committed to, obsessed by and attracted to. Which will tell you what you've got to do, whatever it takes.

(I know this may sound a little extreme, but you've got to realize that "doing what you love" is at the heart and core of every success. Without that, nothing much happens. Want your Dream to become your reality? Then reach down inside yourself and discover what you've got to do. And remember, it has nothing to do with what others want or what you "ought" to do. It's simply who you are and what you know you're here to do and have to do to be happy.)

"Houston, we have liftoff!"

The good news is, when you find what you love to do, you'll also find, in that same moment, the rocket fuel you'll need to propel you past the obstacles you'll have to overcome to make your Dream happen.

"Doing what you love" will give you the fire, energy, passion, and enthusiasm you'll need to keep jumping out of your box, taking chances and working hard.

And you'll need it, too, because willpower alone won't be strong enough to get you through. To succeed, you're going to have to harness the power of what you love and are naturally committed to and use that as the inner power source that drives you on…or you'll quit every time.

So what is "that" for you?

What do you want?

"That," of course, turns out to be the #1 question in life: *"What do you want?"* And the answer to that one simple question has baffled most of us for a very long time.

Ask most people and they'll probably tell you they're "still trying to figure out what they want to be when they grow up." And because most of them, it seems, aren't able to do that, most of them will never get the life they could have had...which is okay, I guess, if they don't mind being another of the walking dead.

But that's not you.

You've come too far to settle for that, and you're ready to know, finally, what your Dream is...because you know you can have it if only you can name it.

So...*what is it?*

And the answer, strangely, is that you already know exactly what it is...but you don't want to know what you know.

(Seems like gibberish, but it's true...it's another case of "us" keeping "us" from getting what we want and could so easily have.)

"I gotta know...don't tell me!"

Psychologist Abe Mazlow called it the "need to know and the fear of knowing."

Which simply means that most of us are dying to know what "it" is...but we don't really want to know because if we do, we'll have to actually do something about it.

So we keep ourselves in the dark.

Powerless. Alone. Less than we could be.

Because if we let ourselves know what our Dream honestly is, we'll have to act on it. And if we act, we may fail. Or tick someone off. Or have to work harder. Or take some risks. Or be forced to stand up to the folks in charge and tell them what we really think. Or end a relationship that's over. Or run the risk of losing "their" love.

And if any of that happens, it'll hurt and probably cause us to look stupid. *(At least that's the way we've got it figured.)*

So our ego – the fake part of us that's usually in charge and determined to look good at all costs – decides it's best *not* to know. Even though *(grab this)* what we're refusing to know is usually the answer we've been looking for all our life. The one we've *got* to have if we're ever going to get out of our box and get what we want!

So how do you let yourself finally "know" what "it" is? Simple: just use the Dream Recovery Process.

(Relax, it's not hard. It'll just take a little time and the willingness to tell yourself the truth, which will be easy because none of this is meant to be shared.)

Remembering What You Want

Step One in recovering your Dream is for you to decide, right now, that it's finally okay to let yourself know what your Dream is.

Why? Because you've now got the power to make it happen!

How do I know?

Easy: you've chosen to be the Master of your own destiny and do whatever it takes to make it happen…and you're not going to give up until it does.

Which means, of course, that it *will* happen…so now it's okay to let yourself know what "it" is.

"But it won't make any money!"

And please don't give me the "I know what I love but I can't make money doing it" routine. That's just another excuse for non-action.

In the real world, people do what they love and make money all the time. Fact is, that's exactly how most wildly successful people get that way: they do what they love and, as a result, make it big…because they're driven to succeed by their own passionate energy.

Without that, they usually quit and find something else to do…and so will you.

Believe me, in this world of six billion people, there's a big-enough market out there for whatever it is you love to do…because there's a market out there for absolutely everything.

Everything!

(And when you're tempted to forget that, remember... most of the so-called "experts" told Picasso his paintings stunk and he'd never sell them. Listen, the "experts" and "critics" will always stand in line to tell you how you'll fail anytime you try and get out of the box and do anything that's new or the least bit different. Ignore them and do it anyway!)

Our job is simple: all we've got to do is find *our* market, let them know we've got what they're looking for and sell a bunch of it.

(That's right, your job is to sell a ton of whatever "it" is and make a great living doing what you love. Forget "getting by" and "just barely making it" and "surviving." Think bigger, shoot higher! You can have a lot more than that! And if any of this strikes you as being the least bit "selfish," find a good therapist and straighten out your thinking because that's just not true. You have every right to live your life your way doing just what you love. And anyone who tells you different is simply wrong.)

But to do that, you've got to get savvy about business. Learn how to market effectively. Become good at selling your wares. All of which is doable because none of it's really all that hard.

Just remember, more than a few potentially bright stars have failed miserably because they thought "selling" was "dirty" and "beneath them" and making money was somehow "crass" or "not spiritual." If you've got that tape playing in your head, erase it now or you'll blow any chance you've got to succeed. Because the reality is, you and I are selling something every day of our lives...whether it's our products, ideas, services, or ourselves.

And we either get very good at it or fail miserably.

Step Two: Now that it's okay to know what your Dream is, you need to begin looking for it by searching for the obvious.

(You'll be amazed at how obvious it was when you finally see it. Remember, too, while you're searching, that your Dream is also trying to find you!)

Think of your Dream as being like my glasses, which I sometimes can't find because they're perched on my head. They're so close, so much a part of me, that I can't see them.

Remember the fish we talked about earlier, who couldn't see the water because it was everywhere? Same thing's true with your Dream. It's so much a part of you and your current life that it's standing right there in front of you, and it's so obvious you may not be able to see it.

What *is* "that" for you?

Step Three: Make sure, for now, that you're only looking for what your Dream is, *not* how you're going to make it happen. Repeat: you're looking for "what," not "how."

I know that sounds simple, but trust me, it's not. One of the biggest reasons most us have a hard time finding our Dream is because we're looking for it in terms of what we think is "possible, doable, reasonable, prudent, and realistic."

Which means we're looking for it *inside* the box we're already living in.

But our Dream is always outside our current box.

It's not about "more of the same, harder." Or what already is. It's about what *can* be! It's about what's new, bold, different, exciting, and what you've always wanted to do. And if you make the mistake of letting your rational in-the-box thinking take over and run your search, you'll never find it.

So for now, focus on just one thing: *what do you want?* We'll deal with *how* to make that happen later.

I promise.

(If you're getting up-tight about any of this, take a deep breath and relax. This whole process is going to happen easier than you ever thought it would. In fact, it's already begun working, even though you're probably not yet aware of it.)

Step Four: Now it's time to ask yourself some questions and to write *(yes, write)* down your answers so they can begin weaving the fabric of your new life. Remember, there are no prizes for making this hard; just tell it like it is for you and don't worry about how you'll make it happen. Ready? Let's begin.

- What do you love to do?
- What would you do even if you weren't getting paid to do it?
- Are you already doing it? How?
- What do you get lost in doing and lose all track of time?
- What are you a natural at?
- What have you been doing most all your life, in one way or another, and it's so much a part of you that you don't even know you're doing it?
- What do people say you're good at? *(I know this is a long list, but hang in and keep writing...it's working.)*
- What's so easy for you to do that you can't understand why others think it's any big deal?
- What daydreams keep floating through your mind and never go away?

- What do you do that gives
  you energy?
- What takes away your energy?
- What makes you smile?
- What makes you happy?
- What makes you sad?
- What did you want to be when
  you grew up?
- If you weren't worried about
  what others might think,
  what would you do?
- If you weren't afraid,
  what would you do?
- If you knew you couldn't fail,
  what would you do?
- What key themes keep repeating
  themselves in your life?

(Please make sure you're writing down your answers. I know it's tempting to just think about them, and that's better than nothing…but the power comes from putting them down on paper. That makes them real; and the more real they are, the more certain they are to happen.)

Step Five: Now ask yourself: what did you love to do when you were a child? Because that's when you probably had a clearer idea of who you were and what you loved and what you wanted to be when you grew up.

Steven Spielberg, for example, loved making home movies when he was a little boy growing up in Arizona and went on to become one of the greatest movie directors in history.

Finding your Dream isn't really all that hard...if you're willing to see the obvious that's trying to happen and admit it and accept it. One of the quickest ways to do that is by remembering what you knew before the "big people" forced you to grow up and be just like them.

(And just for fun, the next time you get together with a bunch of "big people," let yourself see them as the children they used to be. Are they different now? How? Were they more alive then...or now? How much of that's also happened to you? How does that make you feel?)

Step Six: Now convene a conference on *you!* Invite no more than six to eight people who know you well and whose opinion you respect.

(Who you invite is critical. Make certain you ask people who've: 1. Got a bigger box than you do; 2. See more and have different perspectives and insights; and 3. Don't have a vested interest in what you're doing. Do NOT invite the people you normally surround yourself with; most of whom have expectations of you and are only going to support you in "doing your Dream" as long as you keep meeting those expectations. Invite mavericks, heretics, people who see the world differently. Those are the people who can best help you get out of your box. Yeah, they'll make you uncomfortable, but it'll be worth it.)

Ask them to get together with you one evening for no more than two hours to give you their take on what your special gifts are and what they think you ought to be doing with them. Tell them you want their honest opinions and promise you won't be offended.

Before the session begins, have a serious heart-to-heart with yourself and make three firm promises:

1) You *will* stay open, listen hard and not waste everyone's time by justifying *anything*. You're there to listen, not defend.

2) You *will* stay detached, not let yourself get emotionally involved in what's being said, and you refuse to let your feelings get hurt. *(I know that's hard, but for this to work, you've got to stay detached!)* You promise to remember that their opinion is just that: their opinion. Yes, it matters, because it gives you another view of yourself you don't have. But in the end, the only opinion that really matters is yours. *(Re-read that...yes, you want their opinion, but you don't have to take it. Most of what you're going to hear will not work for you, but if you listen hard you'll probably get one or two insights that can change your life.)* So you promise yourself you'll relax and enjoy what they have to say.

3) Finally, you promise you'll keep asking questions and probing deeper until you hear what they're *really* trying to tell you. And you'll have to do that because, without some prodding and pulling, most of them will only tell you what you want to hear because they'll be afraid you'll be offended and won't like, love or respect them anymore. *(People are funny that way...yes, even mavericks and heretics and "strong" people.)*

When the meeting's over, make certain you thank them for the enormous gift they've just given you: their time, sure, but more importantly their ideas and honesty. It's not easy being honest with someone else, even when they ask for it. They came and shared what they thought because they care about you, and they need to hear from you how much you appreciate it and that you care about them as well.

Step Seven: Keep your Dream to yourself!

I know it's tempting to share the Dream that's consuming you with everyone you know, but you'll be a lot better off keeping it to yourself.

Why? Because most people are Certified Dream Killers and don't even know it. And the worst are all those people who love you and want "what's best for you!" Which means, of course, they want you to be just like them.

So when you start telling them about your Dream, and all the "out-of-the-box" things you're going to be doing, they honestly feel it's their "God-given duty" to "set your thinking straight" and get you back in the box with everyone else.

Remember: your Dream is unique, one of a kind and created just for you. It's *not* going to be something anyone else will probably want to do or be or have. So when you discover what it is, you can be certain most everyone you know will probably think you've lost your mind.

(Which means, of course, that you're probably doing it right! Because when everyone else is clapping, that usually means you're becoming "just like them"...and that's a pretty sure sign you're doing it wrong.)

Step Eight: And now (*drum roll, please*) it's finally time to sort through all your notes and thoughts and discoveries and write down your Dream.

Come on, don't get up-tight and make this hard...just write it down simply, in as few words as possible. You know what you want...and if you're still not sure, no problem: just write down what it *would* be if you *did* know...that'll work.

Just make sure your Dream meets three simple criteria: first, that it's what you crave; second, that it's specific, tangible and measurable; and third, that it's *big* enough! Because unless your Dream's bigger than your old box and larger than your old life, it won't have the power you need to turn you on and take you to the next level.

(Here are a few examples: I'll have my own florist shop within three months and it'll be profitable within six months; I'll become a successful writer and sell 5,000 copies of my first book by December; I'll finish my MBA in the next 18 months; we'll move to a small town and I'll spend at least a third of my time enjoying my family and my life; within six months, I'll have a meaningful relationship with someone I love who loves me; I'll be the Senior Vice President of North American Operations one year from today; we'll have built and moved into

the new home we've always wanted within the next 12 months; by next summer, I'll be a successful artist who lives by selling her creations. AGAIN, DON'T MAKE THIS HARD! Just put down what you really want...that's all you've got to do.)

My Dream is: _____

_____

_____

_____

_____

_____

_____

_____

_____

_____

_____

_____

Making it Real

Now that you know what you want, it's time to begin making it real so it can happen more quickly and easily than you ever thought possible.

So find a quiet place where you can be alone for a while, someplace where you won't be disturbed. Now sit back and relax, close your eyes, take a deep breath, and watch as your Dream comes alive on that life-sized movie screen that just opened up inside your mind.

Watch closely as it happens in glorious, living color and listen carefully as the sounds fill your head. Let yourself *feel* what it's like as what you've been dreaming about for so long actually happens...right there in front of you...and now, slowly, gently...step directly into the movie and become a part of it all and experience it fully as it's happening...taking as long as you'd like...enjoying every moment of it.

(This may seem a little strange the first time you do it, but I promise you'll get used to it quickly. And if you're tempted to skip this part of the process because it's too "touchy-feely" or "strange" or might make you look "different," forget it! Because Dreams are like people: they've got to be believed in, fed, worked with, loved, encouraged, and supported...or they'll die. And that's what you're doing here every time you experience your Dream happening: you're feeding it and making it real while, at the same time, growing your belief that you can make it happen. So lighten up and get into it...it'll knock you out how much fun this can be! And remember, the more you do it, the more real your Dream becomes and the quicker it'll happen.)

If you know what you want,
why don't you have it?

So here you are, so close you can taste it.

You know what you want. You can see it happening. You've *felt* it, for God's sake! And you know this Dream you've been thinking about for so long is meant to be yours!

So why isn't it happening?

And the reason, if you're normal, is because you're probably refusing to let your life get that good.

No, most of us don't fail because someone else is doing it to us or stopping us or forcing us to give up. We fail because we stop ourselves. And we do that because some part of us believes getting out of our box and getting what we want will cause us more pain than pleasure.

We're terrified, for example, that we might fail and look stupid. Or be so different from everyone else that "they" won't like us, love us, accept us, or appreciate us anymore.

(Don't laugh...those are the two biggest reasons most of us stop ourselves from getting what we want. I know that sounds silly, but it's true.)

So we unknowingly put a limit on how good we'll let things become before we slam on the brakes and begin sabotaging the very success we've worked so hard to achieve.

And we'll keep doing that until we answer the following two questions and realize, finally, why we've got to let ourselves be outrageously successful *now*.

Freedom!

The first question you need to ask yourself is *What will happen to you if you don't wake up, break out of your box and make your Dream happen?*

You've got to be specific here: what's it going to cost you in terms of self-respect, fulfillment, happiness, and personal satisfaction if you *don't* do this? How much will it cost you financially, now and later? Will you be able to live with yourself if you don't do it?

What *won't* you be able to do in your life? What regrets will you have? How will it impact your health? Will you be more stressed? What kind of role model will you be? What will your kids think of you? What about your spouse or significant other? Your friends? All the people who look up to you?

More importantly, how will you feel about yourself?

(Most of us never realize, until it's too late, how much it'll cost us if we don't do what we know we're here to do. Talk with older people and they'll tell it to you straight: the thing they regret most is playing it too safe and not taking more risks...and now it's too late. You do not want that to happen to you!)

Got it?

Good. Now ask yourself Question #2: *What will you get if you do your Dream?*

Again, you've got to be very specific: how much happier will you be? What will happen to your relationships? What will it do for your health? How much better off will you be financially? What will you now be able to do, be and have?

What new opportunities will you have that you wouldn't have had otherwise? What will you be able to do for your family, your community and your world that you couldn't have done before? What kind of role model will you be?

How will you feel about yourself?

It's your choice

Let's wrap up.

You know what you want.

You know what it'll cost you if you don't do it.

You know what you'll get if you do.

And you know your Dream's only going to happen if you commit completely.

So now the only question left is *will you do it?*

And will you refuse to give up, quit, sell out, wimp out, be like everyone else, play it safe, hold back on your power, let others run your life, do as you're told, be recklessly prudent, or do anything else that turns your life into a giant sucking machine?

If the answer's "yes," check here ❏ and let's get on with making it happen.

And if your answer, for some strange reason, is "no," check here ❏ and listen for the loud slurping sound of failure as all your hopes, Dreams, happiness, satisfaction, and self-respect get sucked down the drain.

(I know I'm being pushy, but I also know your future depends on the choice you make right now. And I'm committed to helping you do whatever it takes to get the happiness you're after. If that makes me pushy, so be it.)

Secret #5: Act Boldly!

"There comes a time to put up or shut up, a time to risk crawling through the window of opportunity as it cracks open in your life. A time to finally let go of what's over and put everything you've got on the line and move on...knowing that's the only way you'll ever get what you really want. When that time came for us, we bought our first business, and I remember pulling out of the driveway that hot, muggy morning, headed for 'greener pastures' in Lubbock, Texas, which had just been hit by a tornado three weeks before. Everything we owned was stashed in a U-Haul truck; we had $800 to our names (the most we could get on our Visa and MasterCard combined); we owed $10,000 in 45 days; my former employer refused to pay my last check; Linda was pregnant with our third child; and an embezzler was discovered working in the business we'd just bought! I think that's when we discovered what it really meant to be bold and committed!"

"Whatever you can do or dream you can, begin it. Boldness has genius, power and magic in it!"
Johann Wolfgang Von Goethe

Y ou've come a long way in a very short time, and I truly admire your courage.

You've made hard choices most people never make *(that's right, never)* as you've learned the Secrets of waking up…remembering who you *really* are…and taking back your power and running your own life.

You've discovered your Dream and chosen not to quit until you make it happen.

But everything you've done up to now, including all the choices you've made, aren't going to make any difference at all unless you *do* the final Secret and *take bold, consistent, nonstop action to turn your good intentions into reality.*

Until you do, nothing's ever going to change, and you and I will have wasted our time together.

Because in the real world, "talk" counts for nothing.

Action is what matters.

And the easiest way to do that is by creating a simple, five-step action plan.

(The key world here is "simple." If your plan's simple, you'll probably do it and it'll work. Make it complicated and it'll probably never happen! Remember, all we're after here is the easiest, fastest, most direct way possible to make your Dream happen. No more, no less.)

So here are the five simple action steps you need to take to change your life:
1) Decide where you're going.
2) See where you are right now.
3) Make a simple plan to get from here to there.
4) Take *bold* action.
5) See if it's working; and if it's not, keep trying something else until it does.

Easy, right? Sure…you can do this!

And to make certain it works, we're going to handle the one thing that'll keep you locked in your old life forever until you face it and deal with it…

…and that's your fear.

"Be afraid! Be very afraid!"

Fear!

That god-awful, gut-wrenching feeling that can easily paralyze you into doing absolutely nothing!

That heart-stopping terror inside you that screams, "I can't do this! I'm gonna throw up; I want my mommy; what the hell am I gonna do; I wanna give up; God save me; I'll lose everything; what's going to happen to me; I'm dying here!"

That's the fear I'm talking about, and it's the biggest reason you don't have what you want.

Where'd it come from?

That steady barrage of enormous and, quite frankly, ridiculous lies you've been fed all your life so you'll stay asleep and keep playing the game like everybody else. Terrible lies that got so brainwashed into your thinking that you're now telling them to yourself as the old tapes play over and over in your head, telling you to "Play it safe."..."Don't take chances."..."Who do you think you are!" ..."Have you lost your mind?"..."It's just not possible!"

All of which is such a huge load of crap!

(So much for being subtle.)

Listen, the truth is you've got *everything* you need to make your Dream come true, and what you don't have, you *can* get. Because the same God that planted that Dream in your Soul also gave you everything else you'll need to pull it off...including all the necessary skills, talents, abilities, resourcefulness, courage, gumption, and smarts.

And they were given to you because your Dream is supposed to happen! *(You need to re-read that.)*

That's why you have it and why you keep feeling the urge to "DO it!"

Sure, you're going to have to show up and do the work. And yes, you'll have to grow and learn and take risks and keep pushing your limits. But the most important thing you've got to do is admit, finally, that the fear that's standing there, blocking your way out of your own private hell...your own little box ...*is not real!*

Yeah, I know it looks *bad!*

And I know everybody tells you it *is* bad!

But the fear is no more real than the bogeyman who used to live under your bed when you were a kid. It's a fraud, a liar, a con man. A paper tiger whose only power lies in the power *you* give it to stop you.

And the easiest way to walk past the fear and get out of your box and get what you want is to *take bold, consistent, nonstop action!*

Day in, day out.

Whether you feel like doing it or not.

Because *action* is the only thing that'll take your fears away and make your Dream come true.

The Secret

But that's the one thing most of us stop doing whenever we feel afraid.

We stop taking action of any kind, much less "bold, massive, nonstop action," and usually choose, instead, to wait to act until our fear goes away and we "*feel* like doing it" *(which, as you well know, seldom happens).*

And so most of us fail…not because we *can't* do it, but because we never learned the simple secret that most successful people use to win big; namely, *they act their way into feeling.*

Which means they make themselves take the action they need to take long before they ever *feel* like doing it…because they know the good feelings that'll keep them going usually come later, *after* they've begun "doing it."

And they also know if they wait to act until they "feel like it," they'll fail most every time.

(The trick is to get off our "buts" and excuses and do what we know we need to do even when we don't feel like doing it. When we do, our fear shrinks and we begin taking even more action and before we know it we've built up a momentum that carries us over the top. No, it's not much harder than that. The question isn't "Can you do it?" That's a given; of course you can do it! The real questions are "Will you do it?" and "When?")

What's your plan?

So keeping that in mind, let's put together a simple, five-step action plan that's got the power to make your Dream come true.

The first thing you need to do? Right, you've got to:

1. Decide where you're going.

This oughta be a no-brainer by now. *(If you're still not sure what you want, you know what to do: just write down what it would be if you did know. That'll work.)*

Now make sure it's specific, tangible and measurable. And finally, be certain it's what you *love* to do and *have* to do, whatever it takes. If it matters to you any less than that, you'll give up when the going gets tough.

And I promise you, it will get tough!

Not just because the game's getting harder, but because most of the people in your life honestly don't want you to win.

(Come on, you knew that! Think about it: they all say they want you to make it, but every time you've gotten the least bit out of the box most of them have tried to stuff you back in...because if you succeed, they'll have to rethink what they've done with their lives and most of them would rather die than do that. It's a lot easier for them to pull you down than build themselves up.)

Here's the Dream I'm going to create, whatever it takes, and my deadline for making it happen *(if you need examples, look back over the ones in Chapter 4 and remember: keep this simple and don't make it hard)*:

_____

_____

_____

_____

2. See where you are right now.

Next, write down where you are right now with regard to getting what you want. If your Dream's to get your MBA, for example, list the prerequisites and see what you'll need to meet them. If you're going to start your own business, list everything it'll take and see what you've got and what you need to come up with. Want a better job? Like to travel the world? Desire a more meaningful relationship? Same drill: what'll it take, what have you got and what do you need to come up with? The point here is to get real about where you are right now in relation to getting what you want.

(Wherever you're at right now is perfect, so don't let yourself get discouraged. We've all got to start some-where, and the only thing that matters is that you can do this!)

Here's where I'm at right now relative to making my Dream happen: _____

_____

_____

_____

3. Make a simple plan to get from here to there.

Step Three is to come up with the *quickest* and *easiest* way to get what you want, and one of the best ways to do that is by finding someone who's already doing your Dream and asking them to tell you how they made it happen.

Why? Two reasons:

First, the *quickest* way to get out of your box and get what you want is to run with, hang with, spend time with people who have a bigger box than you do. There's just no easier way to break through the walls in your own mind that are stopping you from getting what you want and becoming wildly successful.

Second, it's dumb to waste your time, money and effort trying to reinvent the wheel when there's one out there that already works! Dump your ego and your need to be right and your obsession with being "the one who knows!"…and do this the easy way: listen and learn and let those who've done it show you how to tiptoe through the minefield so you make it easily and successfully to the other side.

The good news is they're dying to tell you exactly that!

They *want* to be asked and they're willing to tell you most everything you need to know if you'll swallow your pride and get up a little courage and go ask them.

Your job right now?

Write down the names of three people who are living all or part of your Dream, find a way to get in touch with each of them and ask them to tell you how they did it.

That's it!

(Don't let this throw you...it's totally doable. You just have to get resourceful and be persistent and find a way to make contact. It will happen if you decide to make it happen.)

And to make certain your time with them is as productive as possible, make sure you:

- park your ego before you meet and spend your time focusing on *them.*
- list and ask them every question you can possibly think of and, with their permission, take detailed notes.
- honor their time and, when it's up, ask if you can call them again.
- offer to help them in any way you can.
- make certain you send them a personal follow-up note that day, thanking them for their help and promising to keep in touch and let them know what happens *(then make certain you do it).*

Now go back through your notes and ask yourself, given this reality check, if you still believe your Dream's real and doable.

If the answer's "Yes," decide which parts of what they're doing will work for you, put those together with the other pieces you've come up with and create your own personal success plan…complete with a list of giant steps you'll need to take to make that plan work.

Now break down each of those giant steps into small, doable baby steps, prioritize them, set firm deadlines, and make yourself get them done, one by one…rewarding yourself for every step you take along the way.

(And while you're doing this, remember: your Dream's right here waiting for you to make it real, but the only way it's ever going to happen is if you name it, claim it, make a plan, and get on with getting it done. Anything else is wishful thinking.)

Here's my plan, complete with deadlines *(yes, you'll need a lot more paper)*: _____

_____

_____

_____

_____

_____

_____

4. Take bold action!
(Hang on, we're almost done....)

You know what you want, where you are now relative to getting it, and you've got a workable plan...but it'll remain a pipedream until you take *bold, consistent, nonstop action* to make it happen.

Halfhearted efforts, tentatively done, won't get you anywhere. "Trying" is no better than dying. If your Dream's ever going to happen, you're going to have to go for it full-out in a big way or forgetaboutit.

Which means?

You've got to take big, bold, out-of-the-box actions that will cause you to stand out and get seen and heard in this overcrowded world of look-alikes as the sole source supplier of what your best customers want and need most in a way that's not easily duplicated by your competition.

Or, to put it more simply, you've got to find a way to be unique and shine the spotlight on yourself and what you're offering.

A way to help people see that you've got what they've been looking for.

And that means giving up any illusions you've got that "playing it safe" and "being careful" and keeping a low profile will ever get you what you want.

BOLDNESS is what it takes to succeed in today's media-blitzed world – you either find a way to stand out or you go nowhere. I don't care whether you're building a business, getting a better job, saving the environment, or finding a mate: boldness, putting yourself out there and taking center stage is what it takes.

And if that scares you, relax; you're normal. It scares most of us.

The secret is to have the fear and go ahead and do it anyway. *(Yes, you can.)*

Two final suggestions:

First, don't spend all your time looking at "the big picture" because you can easily get overwhelmed. Trekking in Nepal taught me a better way: just get on the trail every day and keep taking the next step and, before you know it, you're at the top. Dreams, like mountain climbing, don't happen overnight. So pick one part, one area, one step that will move you closer to getting your Dream and get it done, one small step at a time.

Second, ignore that screaming voice inside your head that keeps telling you to "play it safe" and "don't burn your bridges," because both of those are great prescriptions for failure.

Sure, you'll need to make some sort of orderly transition from your old life to your new one…but there'll come a time when you'll finally have to let go of your old life and commit to your new one. And at that moment, you'll need to remember Caesar, who marched his reluctant troops into battle on an island – and then burned the only bridge back to the mainland.

And Cortez, who taught his soldiers what it meant to be committed by burning all the ships after they landed in the New World.

Now it's your turn!

These are three bold actions I'll take to make my Dream happen, along with the dates by which each of them will be done: _____

_____

_____

_____

_____

_____

_____

_____

_____

5. See if it's working; and if it's not, keep trying something else until it does.

You know the definition of "insanity," right? That's when you keep doing the same thing and expect to get different results. Well, that pretty well sums up how most of us spend our lives. Not getting the results we want? Hey, no problem...we'll just keep doing what's not working, but this time we'll do it harder, faster, with more style, money, class, etc.

Fundamentally change what we're doing and try something else? "No way!" we scream. "I've done it this way all my life and I'm gonna keep doin' it till it works!"

(Talk about being locked in a box!)

To make your Dream happen, you're going to have to use a different strategy, and it works like this: if what you're doing isn't getting you what you want, you're going to have to change what you're doing and keep trying one new thing after another until you find a way that works.

If you never give up, you have to succeed!

(It's like taking a ring of keys and trying them, one after another, until you find one that opens the lock. It's not hard...it just takes time and the willingness to keep trying new things.)

And when you forget how easy all this is, think about the little kid in the grocery store who pitches a fit, whines, cries, pleads, begs, and finally sits quietly in the shopping cart…whatever it takes to get his mom to buy him the candy he's after.

Do you think he's worried about how he looks? Or what anyone else thinks about him or what he's doing? Is he afraid of failing? Does he fear rejection? You know he doesn't! All he wants is the candy, and he knows he'll get it if he just keeps doing whatever it takes to make it happen.

Go ye and do likewise!

(I mean, come on. How hard is this? You and I have been doing this "candy thing" since we were kids. We're experts at it! But most of us have over-grown up and aren't willing anymore to do whatever it takes to "go for the candy." Sadly, most of us are losing our heart's desire simply because we don't want to look bad. We're afraid "they" might not like us anymore, so we hold back and fail. How dumb is that?)

Here are five different out-of-the-box ways I can also make my Dream come true *(don't slack off and BS your way through this…the ways you're going to list here will probably wind up being the very ones that'll save you)*:

_____

_____

_____

_____

_____

_____

_____

Now What?

So that's it. Getting what you want is as simple as waking up, remembering who you really are, taking back your power, following your Dream, and taking bold, consistent, nonstop action to make it happen.

Can you do that?

Of course you can...the only real question is *will* you? What *will* you do with what you've learned and the decisions you've made?

Unless you're very careful, the answer is "not much."

Why?

Because there's a very real possibility you may give in to the temptation to sit back and "think about all this" instead of making a plan and taking bold, meaningful, nonstop action to make it happen.

Unless you act *now*, your old brainwashing will re-wrap it's slimy tentacles around your thinking and, before you know it, you'll be back asleep, trying to fit in and be like everybody else.

And you'll give up.

Quit.

Blow off your Dream.

And justify it with a bunch of perfectly "good" reasons why you "really can't do it"…and they'll make "good sense"…at least to you.

You know, you'll be "too busy," have too much work to do, need to take a break and watch TV, have a beer with some friends, buy groceries, do the laundry, cut your grass, trim your nails, get the car washed.

All that important stuff that's "just *gotta* get done!"

You'll tell yourself you'll get to your Dream "later," when you "get some time" and "feel like it."

But later, of course, will never come and before you know it, you'll be right back where you were when you bought this book. But now you'll feel worse…because you'll know you failed yourself and missed your chance to live… to really *live!*

And you'll regret it till the day you die.

Why do I care?

Because we're talking about your life here!

This isn't some academic theory or cute little book full of happy-talk about some imaginary Dream. We're talking about *you* and what happens to you for the rest of your life.

You're damn right I care!

And there's no way I'm going to let you go back to sleep and not follow through and do whatever it takes to make your Dream come true. Because I know it's in you to do it, and I know you can do it, and I know you've got to do it to be happy.

All you've got to do is take it one step at a time and get it done!

So tell me, what are you going to do first?

Perfect.

What are you going to do next?

Excellent.

And after that?

Dead-on.

Yeah, I know. I'm being pushy again.

But I didn't write this book just to keep you entertained.

I wrote it because I know who you are, and I'm committed to making sure you wake up and remember your own greatness...committed to making sure you take back your power, follow your Dreams and actually *live* before you die.

And I'm *not* going to give up until that happens!

So get to it, and let me know how you're doing. You can always find me at www.patlynch.com.

And when it's hard and things aren't working out the way you'd planned or you're feeling stuck or you've blown it bigtime and want to quit, read this and know I'm always here, urging you on...because I *know* you can do this!

Keep on!

There's good news and bad news.
Ups and downs.
You feel good and you feel rotten.
People come and people go.
They love you and they hate you.
You feel like doing it and then you don't.

No matter...it's all just part of the game.

And through all the laughter and tears,
the only thing that gets you through is
keeping your will clear, your feelings
under control and staying focused on
your purpose.

On what you know you've got to do.

Not because someone else said you had to,
ought to or should want to. But because
your Soul, who you really are, knows what
you've got to do and it told you so.
In a quiet voice you could no longer deny.

So you keep on keeping on.

It rains, no problem...you keep on.
The sun shines, you laugh...and keep on.
They love you, you smile...and keep on.
They hate you, you shrug...and keep on.

They think you're a genius, you grin…and keep on.
They think you're a fool, you chuckle…and keep on.
They clap loudly, you take a bow…and keep on.
They boo and criticize, you ignore them…and keep on.
They think you're great, you agree…and keep on.
They think you're an idiot, you don't care…and you
keep on.

Because what "they" think or do no longer starts
or stops you.
Sure, it hurts. Sure, it feels good.
But you know the game's not about how you feel.
It's about what you know you've got to do.

Which has nothing to do with "them."
And everything to do with you.
And the Dream inside that pulls you on
and has to be done.
Or your life will have been a complete waste.

So you keep on.

Not because you have to. Or someone told you to.
No, you do your Dream because you know
you've got to.
Like it or not.
Good news or bad news.
It's who you are. It's what you do.
And your days are good.

Because through it all, win or lose,
you keep choosing to be true to yourself.
To keep believing.
And to never give up.

Pat

Share The Five Secrets With Others

To order copies:

Visit our website: http://www.potentialpress.com
E-mail: orders@potentialpress.com
Call: 1-800-404-8121
Fax this order form to: 1-928-445-0074
Mail: Potential Press, 1042 Willow Creek Rd.,
Suite A-101-250, Prescott, AZ 86301, USA.

Bulk Sales

For special discounts on bulk purchases or to learn how your organization may use this book and include your message in a customized version, e-mail: information@potentialpress.com. Special books/excerpts can be created to meet unique needs.

Please send the following:

❑ The Five Secrets @ $19.95 U.S. Qty. ___
❑ You Can, Too! Success Stories @ $19.95 U.S. Qty. ___
❑ The Five Secrets Companion Journal @ $14.95 U.S. Qty.___
❑ The Five Secrets Audio CD @ $14.95 U.S. Qty. ___

Name:_____

Address:_____

City: _____ State: ___ Zip:_____

Telephone:_____

E-mail address: _____

Sales tax: Please add 6.3% for products shipped to Arizona addresses.
Shipping by air: U.S.: $4.00 for first product; $2.00 each additional.
International: $9.00 first product; $5.00 each additional (estimate).

Payment: ❑ Visa ❑ MasterCard (No checks, cash, COD)

Card number: _____

Name on card:_____ Exp. date:_____

Signature: _____

Share The Five Secrets With Others

To order copies:

Visit our website: http://www.potentialpress.com
E-mail: orders@potentialpress.com
Call: 1-800-404-8121
Fax this order form to: 1-928-445-0074
Mail: Potential Press, 1042 Willow Creek Rd.,
Suite A-101-250, Prescott, AZ 86301, USA.

Bulk Sales

For special discounts on bulk purchases or to learn how your organization may use this book and include your message in a customized version, e-mail: information@potentialpress.com. Special books/excerpts can be created to meet unique needs.

Please send the following:

❑ The Five Secrets @ $19.95 U.S. Qty. ___
❑ You Can, Too! Success Stories @ $19.95 U.S. Qty. ___
❑ The Five Secrets Companion Journal @ $14.95 U.S. Qty.___
❑ The Five Secrets Audio CD @ $14.95 U.S. Qty. ___

Name:_____

Address:_____

City: _____ State:___ Zip:_____

Telephone:_____

E-mail address: _____

Sales tax: Please add 6.3% for products shipped to Arizona addresses.
Shipping by air: U.S.: $4.00 for first product; $2.00 each additional.
International: $9.00 first product; $5.00 each additional (estimate).

Payment: ❑ Visa ❑ MasterCard (No checks, cash, COD)

Card number: _____

Name on card:_____ Exp. date:_____

Signature: _____

About The Author

Pat Lynch is a leading authority on change and has used the power of the Five Secrets for the last four decades to make his dreams come true.

He's owned a variety of businesses, established graduate and undergraduate programs, run campaigns, turned around companies and organizations, and presented more than 1,000 programs, workshops and seminars around the world. He's also worked in the inner city, been a foster parent, father, grandfather, columnist, and consultant.

Pat lives in Arizona and Mexico with Linda, his wife and partner for the last thirty-nine years. He may be reached at www.patlynch.com.